DO

MARIAROSA GUERRINI O.S.A.

DO YOU LOVE ME?

ST PAULS

Original title: *Mi ami tu?* produced by the Federation of
Augustinian Nuns, Italy.
First published in 1984 by Editrice Rogate Roma.

Translated by Vincent Siletti SSP
English text lettering by Mary Lou Winters FSP
Texts from the Gospels have been freely translated and,
in places, adapted.

ST PAULS Publishing
187 Battersea Bridge Road, London SW11 3AS, UK

ISBN 0854392 475

Printed by Interprint Ltd., Marsa, Malta

ST PAULS is an activity of the priests and brothers of the
Society of St Paul who proclaim the Gospel through the
media of social communication

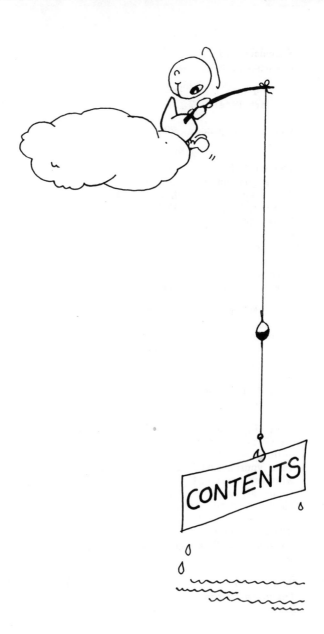

DO YOU LOVE ME ?

LIFE
HAS ALWAYS BEEN A STORY OF LOVE .

ONE **LIVES**
IN THE MEASURE THAT ONE **LOVES** .

DO YOU LOVE ME ?

WE HAVE TRIED
-AND HOPE WE HAVE SUCCEEDED-
TO OFFER YOU
A SMILING GLIMPSE
OF **TRUE LOVE**
THROUGH THE SIMPLICITY
OF THIS LITTLE BOOK .

READING ITS PAGES
"THOSE WHO HAVE BEEN CALLED"
WILL RECOGNIZE THEMSELVES,
AND EVERYONE WILL BE ABLE
TO GRASP THE CRITERION
AND THE MEASURE
OF TRUE AND REAL LOVE .

THE AUGUSTINIAN NUNS

PROLOGUE

In the **heart** of every human being
the Creator
has written a **call**.
The answer to it
is the secret of true joy.
For some
the call is radical,
totalitarian,
to the point of
giving one's life.

The Twelve, the First,
know something about it.......!
We asked Peter,
who experienced the
unutterable joy (cf 1 Pt 1,8)
of the answer,
to describe for us
the fascinating adventure
of **FOLLOWING** Jesus,
to proclaim to us
the sweeping message
of the Lord's teaching
which changed the Twelve
-simple, rough people that they were -

into men disposed to everything,
free and peace-loving,
pillars of Christ's Church
and of His Truth.

The story of Peter
is the story of impassioned love,
unique.

Jesus Himself
had expected it of Peter.
And it was only
on this condition that
Peter could have **FOLLOWED** Jesus;
only on this condition
Jesus would have entrusted to Peter
all those
for whom
He had come
to give Himself,
life.

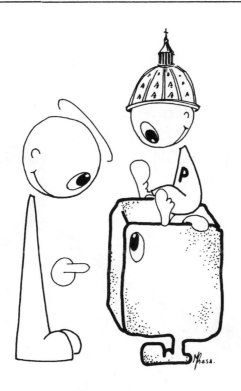

YOU ARE PETER

the Rock
upon which I will build
my Church.
Mt. 16, 18

To you
I shall give
the keys of the
KINGDOM OF
HEAVEN

WHO IS THIS JESUS ?

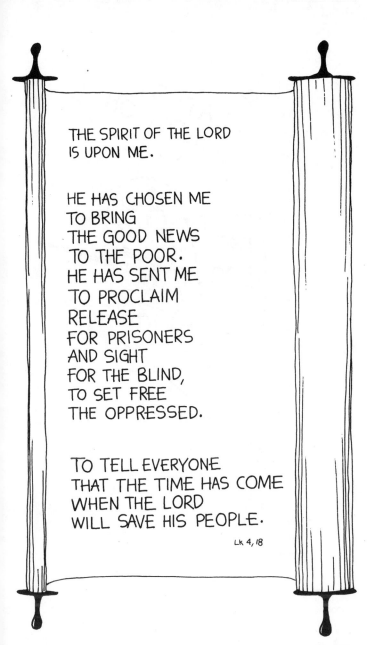

THE SPIRIT OF THE LORD
IS UPON ME.

HE HAS CHOSEN ME
TO BRING
THE GOOD NEWS
TO THE POOR.
HE HAS SENT ME
TO PROCLAIM
RELEASE
FOR PRISONERS
AND SIGHT
FOR THE BLIND,
TO SET FREE
THE OPPRESSED.

TO TELL EVERYONE
THAT THE TIME HAS COME
WHEN THE LORD
WILL SAVE HIS PEOPLE.

Lk 4, 18

23

27

THE CALL:

I have seen
his greatness
with my own eyes (cf 2 Pt 1, 16)

He has travelled
our roads
telling us about a *new life*.
(cf 2 Pt 1, 3·10)

He has called us
out of darkness
to lead us
into his wonderful light (cf 1 Pt 2, 9)

And we
followed Him.

And you, too,
try not to forget
that God has chosen you
and has called you (cf 2 Pt 1, 3·10)

PETER
Apostle of Jesus

AND THEY stayed with Him...

Jn 1, 39

WHAT A LOVELY DAY
THEY HAD,
WHAT A LOVELY NIGHT!

Let us, too, start
building in our hearts
a home where the Lord
can come, and teach us,
and stay
to talk with us.

St. Augustine, Comment. Jn 7, 9

He saw a man sitting
in the customs house
(his name was MATTHEW) and said to him:

And he rose
   and FOLLOWED HIM.
Mt 9,9

ONE DAY.......

He called his disciples to Him
and chose twelve of them,
and called them His
APOSTLES.

LK 6, 13

He called those
whom He held in His heart,
those whom He had chosen
because they were responsive
to His plan.

(Cardinal Martini, "Bible and Vocation")

37

HE CALLED US
SO THAT WE WOULD
STAY WITH HIM

cf Mk 3,14

STAY WITH HIM

We were to see
what Jesus did,
to live with Him,
and then
take Him to others,
and to reproduce Him:
we were to reproduce
His presence.

(Cardinal Martini "Bible and Vocation")

AND ALSO
TO GO OUT TO
PROCLAIM HIS GOOD NEWS.

cf MK 3, 14

THE DIFFICULT.......
.......BUT STIMULATING

CATECHISM
OF
JESUS

He began to send us out
in pairs
to proclaim the Kingdom of God –
and told us: Lk 9,1

If in any place
they do not welcome you
and will not listen to you, ...

as you go away,
shake off the dust
from under your feet!

Mk 6,11

ANYONE
WHO WELCOMES YOU
WELCOMES ME

Mt 10, 40

45

47

Whoever stands
on the "mountain-top"
to speak aloud...
is more exposed
to be a "target"...

What I tell you in whispers

shout from the housetops...
Mt 10, 27

WHAT YOU HAVE RECEIVED AS A GIFT,

GIVE AS A GIFT.

Mt 10,8

I have given you power
to trample on snakes
and scorpions,

NOTHING
WILL DO YOU
HARM·

LK 10,17

DO NOT BE AFRAID!

The very hairs
of your head
are all counted...

Mt 10, 30

53

To be near Jesus,
to follow Him,
was an exciting adventure.
It was not something
just for anybody.

His were hard expectations:
it required courage
and the strength of a wrestler,
but it had a fascinating
influence on us,
and not only
on us Twelve
because by now
many were those
who followed Him!

FOLLOWING HIM

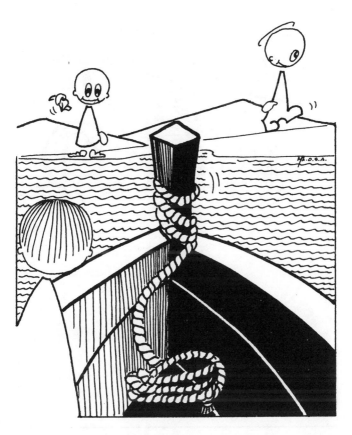

LEAVE EVERYTHING BEHIND

Your security,
your efficiency,
... your rationality...

Jesus said to him:

" Foxes have their holes,
and the birds of the air their nests,
but the SON OF MAN HAS NOWHERE
TO LAY HIS HEAD"

Lk 9, 57

NO ONE
WHO HAS PUT
HIS HAND TO THE PLOUGH
AND LOOKS BACK ...

IS FIT
FOR THE
KINGDOM
OF GOD.

Lk 9, 62

If a man
wishes to come after me,
let him deny himself,

TAKE UP
HIS CROSS...

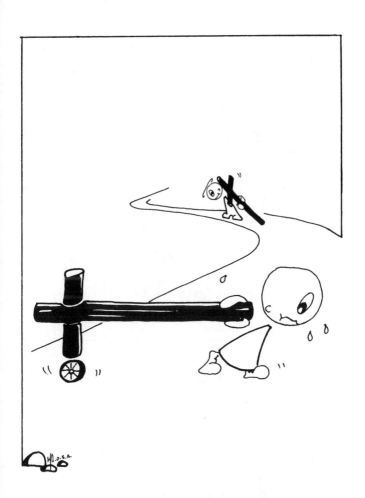

... AND FOLLOW ME.

MH 16, 24

LOVE YOUR CROSS!

Whoever
cannot see his journey's goal
let him fasten himself upon the CROSS
and it
will carry him.

St. Augustine, Comment. on Jn 2,2

WHOEVER LOSES
his life
for my sake
will find it.

Mt 16, 25

65

THERE WAS SOMEBODY WHO SAID NO.......

But he,
when he heard those words,
went away sad,
because he was very rich···

Mt 19, 16

72

ONE DAY.......

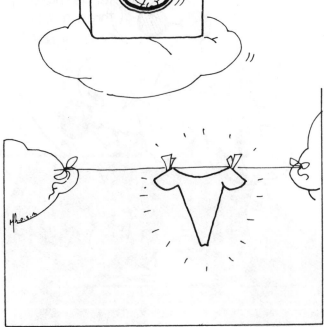

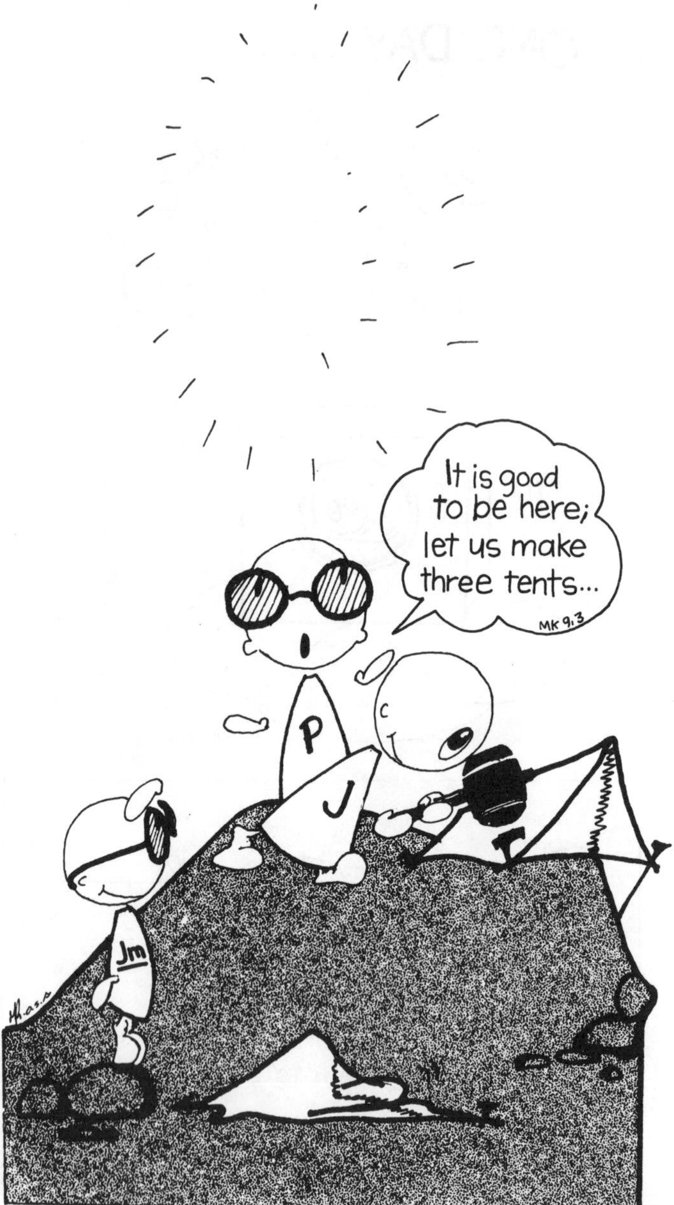
It is good to be here; let us make three tents...
MK 9.3
P
J
Jm

BUT........

CAMPING
"Three Tents"

COME DOWN, PETER.
You wished to have a rest
up on the mountain;
but no;
come down;...
come down to earth to work,
to serve,
to be scorned,
to be crucified.

St Augustine, Discourse 78, 6

When you pray,
go into your room,
and shut the door,

PRAY TO YOUR FATHER
IN SECRET.

Mt 6, 6

PRAY
WITHOUT CEASING
because:

If you ask,
you will receive;

if you seek,
you will find;

if you knock,
the door will be
opened to you...

Mt 7, 7

WHERE
TWO OR THREE
ARE GATHERED TOGETHER
IN MY NAME

I AM THERE

IN THE MIDST

OF THEM.

Mt 18, 20

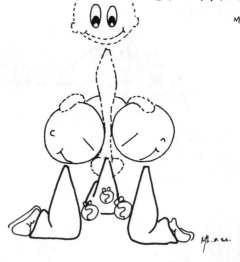

an
UNSHAKABLE
FAITH...

...CLEAR
AND FEARLESS !!!

If your faith is
even as big as a mustard-seed,

you will move
mountains...   Mt 17,20

If you had faith
as big as a mustard-seed,
you could say to this mulberry tree:
 "Pull out your roots....

... and plant them in the sea!"

Lk 17,6

86

... a
CLEAR,
UNTROUBLED
TRUST...

Do not be anxious
about the food you need,
nor about clothes for your body...

EVERY DAY
HAS ENOUGH TROUBLES
OF ITS OWN!

Mt 6, 36

LOOK AT
THE BIRDS OF THE AIR:

they do not sow, or reap...
yet, your Father in heaven
looks after them...   Mt 6,26

LOOK AT
THE LILIES OF THE FIELD:

they do not work, they do not spin...
and yet, not even Solomon,
in all his glory,
was dressed as splendidly
as one of these!

Mt 6, 29

I GIVE YOU A NEW COMMANDMENT:

LOVE
ONE ANOTHER

From this
everyone will know
that you are my disciples...

Jn 13, 34

THERE IS NO GREATER PROOF
OF LOVE THAN THIS:

TO LAY DOWN
YOUR LIFE
FOR THOSE YOU LOVE.

Jn 15,13

... ALSO

If a grain
of wheat
does not die,
it remains a single grain, ...

but
if it dies,
then it produces
many grains.

Jn 12, 24

AND...

When you have done all that you have been given to do, you must say:

WE ARE BUT WORTHLESS SERVANTS.

LK 17, 10

None of us
had ever heard anyone
speak like Jesus.

His Message
gave you all the
motives to live for.....

You learned
a new wisdom
that gave meaning
to life.

To you
it has been given
to understand the mysteries
of the Kingdom of God;
but for the others
they have been put in parables,
so that,

> *They may look but not see*
> *and hear but not understand.*
> Lk 8, 10

THE KINGDOM OF HEAVEN

... is like

a man looking for
fine pearls;

he finds one pearl
of great value,
and goes and
sells all that he has
and buys it.

Mt 13, 45

... may be likened to

... a field
with good seed
and weeds ... Mt 13,24

Every plant
not planted by my
Father in heaven
will be rooted out.
Mt 15, 13

THE KINGDOM OF HEAVEN

...may be likened to
one who has sown seed:

the person who fails
to understand
the Word of God
is like the seed
that fell by the wayside ...

the seed that fell
on rocky ground
is like the person who
has no roots,
an inconstant person ...

the seed that fell
among briars means
the person who
listens to the Word,
but is stifled by worldly cares
and attractions...

the seed sown in good soil
means the person
who listens to the Word,
and understands it,
and bears
fruit...

Cf Mt 13,18

LORD,
you entrusted me with
5 talents; see I have
made a further 5 ....

LORD, you entrusted me with 2 talents;
see, I have made a further 2 ....

LORD, you entrusted me
with 1 talent; I was afraid,
and hid it away under ground...

**TO HIM WHO HAS PLENTY,
MORE WILL BE GIVEN,**
BUT FROM HIM WHO HAS LITTLE
EVEN WHAT HE HAS
WILL BE TAKEN AWAY.
Mt 25.20

EVERYONE WHO LISTENS
to my words
and obeys them
is like a wise man
Who built his house
on rock.

Mt 7, 24

EVERYONE WHO LISTENS
to my words
and does not obey them,
is like a foolish man
who built his house
upon sand ...

BE WATCHFUL!

Because you do not know
on what day
the Lord is coming. Mt 24, 42

YOU
ARE THE SALT
OF THE EARTH

Mt 5,13

YOU ARE THE LIGHT
OF THE WORLD

Mt 5,14

The lamp of the body is the eye;
if your eye is sound,
your whole body will be full of light;

but if your eye is not healthy,
your whole body
will be in darkness.

Mt 6, 22

WHOEVER FOLLOWS ME......

WILL NOT WALK
IN DARKNESS...

Jn 8,12

COME TO ME

AND

I WILL GIVE YOU REST.

Mt 11, 28

WHOEVER IS THIRSTY

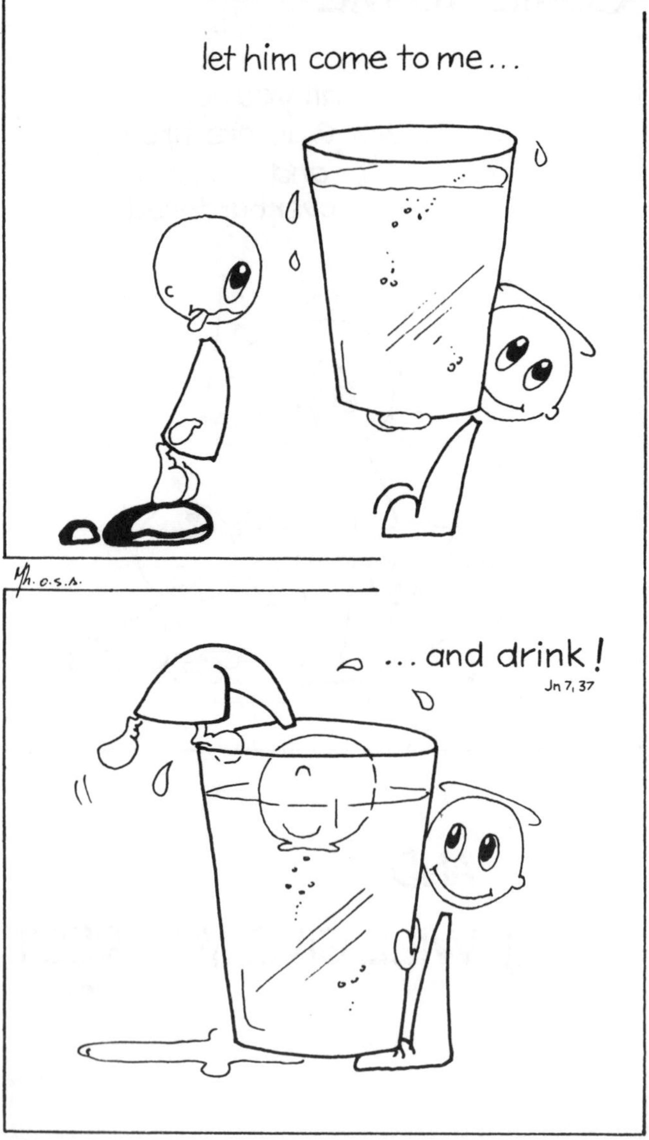

The measure
you use for others
will be used
for you in return...

Mt 7,2

If someone takes away
your cloak,
do not refuse him your tunic.

Lk 6, 29

If anyone slaps you
on the right cheek,

offer him the other cheek.   Mt 5,39

AND NO REQUITAL!

LOVE
 YOUR
  ENEMIES

Mt 5, 44

THERE WILL BE
MORE REJOICING IN HEAVEN
OVER ONE SINNER WHO REPENTS
than over 99 people
who have no need of repentance...
Lk 15, 7

He was UNCOMPROMISING...

but we followed Him
with eagerness
simply because He was like that...

We felt we had
been launched into a
wonderful adventure...

Enter
by the narrow door
that leads to life...

Mt 7, 13

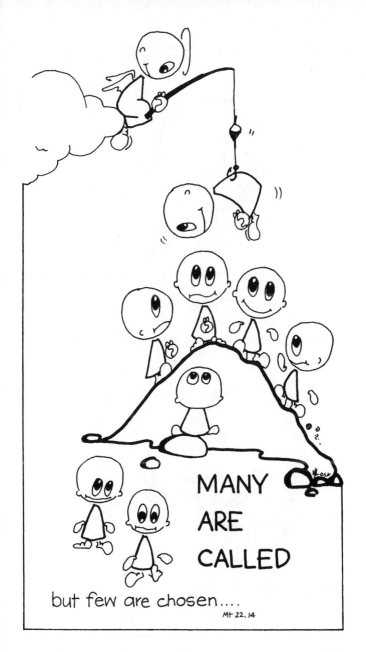

MANY
ARE
CALLED

but few are chosen....

Mt 22, 14

RENDER TO CAESAR the things that are Caesar's...

To Caesar the coins,
to God your selves.
And the Truth will be reproduced in us.

St Augustine, Comment. 40, 9

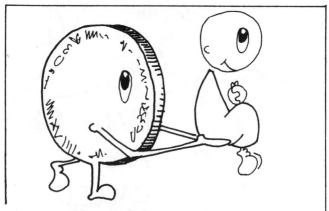

AND TO GOD
the things that are God's. Mt 6, 21

YOU CANNOT SERVE BOTH

GOD
AND
MONEY

Mt 6, 24

It is easier
for a camel to enter
through the eye of a needle...

...than for a rich man
to enter the Kingdom of God.

Mt 19, 24

LORD, IF THAT IS SO...

OF YOU I DEMAND
SINCERITY...

Let your word be plain
Yes when you mean **Yes**
No when you mean **No**

anything beyond this
is from the evil one...
Mt 5, 37

If your right eye
causes you to sin,
pluck it out,
throw it away!... Mt 5.29

and if your hand
causes you to sin,
chop it off
and throw it away... Mt 5.30

BETTER FOR YOU
that one part of your body should perish,
than that the whole
of it go into hell !

Mt 5, 30

AND BE CAREFUL...

whoever
scandalizes little ones...
it would better for that person to...

Mt: 18, 6

BEWARE OF THE PHARISEES...

THEY DO NOT PRACTISE
WHAT THEY PREACH.

They bind heavy burdens
and pile them on other
people's shoulders,
but themselves never lift a finger
to move them.
Mt 23, 3

WOE TO YOU...

BLIND GUIDES

you strain off gnats

and swallow camels!

Mt 23, 24

WOE TO YOU...

Scribes and Pharisees! Hypocrites!
you clean
the outside of cup and dish,

when inside it is full
of your greed and wickedness.
Mt 23.25

WOE TO YOU...

WHITEWASHED
SEPULCHRES !

Mt 23, 27

... But
above everything else
Jesus loved one thing:

HUMILITY.

Perhaps because the humble
were more like Him,
and let Him say and do things
because
they trusted Him.

TAKE
MY YOKE
UPON YOU

AND LEARN FROM ME
FOR I AM
MEEK
AND HUMBLE OF HEART...

Mt 11,29

MY YOKE
        IS GENTLE
AND MY BURDEN
        LIGHT...

Mt 11, 30

IF ANYONE WANTS TO BE
FIRST...

LET HIM BE
LAST OF ALL
AND THE SERVANT
OF ALL !

Mk 9, 35

WHOEVER EXALTS HIMSELF
WILL BE HUMBLED,

WHOEVER HUMBLES HIMSELF
WILL BE EXALTED.

Mt 23, 11

HUMILITY IS THE STEP

St Augustine, Comment 96, 3, 3

Sometimes
we were jealous
of one another.

We wanted to know
if the fact that
one had been longer with Jesus
was being
taken into account or not.

In short, we wanted to know
WHICH OF US

WAS THE GREATEST...

BUT JESUS:

(cf Guardini, "The Lord")

THE ELDEST

**AMONG YOU
MUST BE LIKE
THE YOUNGEST.**

Mt 22, 26

WHOEVER BECOMES
LITTLE
LIKE A CHILD

WILL BE
THE GREATEST
IN THE KINGDOM
OF HEAVEN.

Lk 9, 48

149

IF YOU DO NOT BECOME
LIKE LITTLE CHILDREN...

REMAIN
WELL FOUNDED
IN THE WORDS
I HAVE
SPOKEN
TO YOU.

cf Jn 8, 32

And my TRUTH

WILL SET YOU FREE *!!!*..

How many more things
Jesus told us,
and what great joys
and sorrows
we shared with Him...!

And always
He was with us
giving strength,
especially when
there was the first
glimpse of sadness
for what was to happen
to Him
and when the hour
of separation
was drawing near...

JERUSALEM

If they remain silent,
the very stones
will cry out! Lk 19, 40

DO NOT LET
YOUR HEARTS
BE TROUBLED.

Jn 14, 27

REMAIN IN ME...

I AM THE VINE
YOU ARE
THE BRANCHES

Whoever remains in me
and I in him,
will bear much fruit,
for
WITHOUT ME
YOU CAN DO
NOTHING.

Jn 15,1

YOU WILL HAVE TO SUFFER IN THIS WORLD...

I HAVE CONQUERED THE WORLD!

Jn 16,3

THE HOUR HAS COME

Father, ...
The glory
which you gave me,
I have given to them,
that
THEY MAY BE ONE
AS WE ARE ONE.

Jn 17,22

ALL IS FULFILLED

Jn 19, 30

Peter
had denied Jesus,
but *loved* Him.

Presumption
had exalted him,
denial
had humbled him,
tears
had washed him clean...

It was in fact
necessary
that Christ should first die
for the salvation of Peter,

so that Peter,
in turn,
could die
for the Gospel of Christ.

NOW IS THE MOMENT, PETER,

when you must
no longer fear death,
because the one
whose death you mourned
now lives ...

Now
that He has paid
for your ransom
you can **FOLLOW**
your Redeemer,
and follow Him
without reserve
even to the
death on the cross.

St Augustine. Comment. 123, 4

THE FIRST DAY
AFTER THE SABBATH...

I ran to the tomb
and... LK 24.1

THE GREATEST JOY
OF MY LIFE:

AND WAS TAKEN UP TO HEAVEN... Mt 16, 19

Jesus ascended into heaven,
may our hearts
rise with Him...

St Augustine, Discourse on the Ascension

PENTECOST...

... SO AS NOT TO LEAVE US ALONE...

GO OUT TO
THE WHOLE WORLD
AND PROCLAIM
THE GOOD NEWS

TO EVERY CREATURE!

Mk 16.15

Go everywhere
to declare that **GOD**
LOVES EVERYONE

Acts 20,24

HEAVEN
AND EARTH
WILL PASS AWAY,
BUT MY WORDS
WILL NEVER PASS AWAY.

Mt 24, 35

I AM
WITH YOU
ALWAYS
EVEN TO
THE END
OF THE
WORLD

Mt 28, 20

BE BRAVE !

I AM
YOUR
FAN

cf St Augustine, Discourse 344

Publisher's note

This little book,
on the theme of
the call of the Gospel to
follow Christ
in a life of love,
has been produced
and published by
the priests and brothers
of the Society of St Paul
and the Daughters of St Paul,
two of the Congregations of
the Pauline Family whose mission
is to proclaim the Gospel
all over the world
through the media of
social communication .

next:

LATE HAVE I LOVED YOU

ST AUGUSTINE

a man for God....
a man for man